Wednesday's
P·R·A·Y·E·R

A Father's Guide
to Praying and Fasting
For His Children

STEVE CHAPMAN

Except where noted, scripture quotations in this book are taken from
the New American Standard Bible.

Cover photo and design: Ed Maksimowicz

Special thanks to Dr. David Harrell for his editing and wise counsel.

Library of Congress Cataloging-in-Publication Data
Chapman, Steve
Wednesday's Prayer-A Father's Guide To Praying and Fasting
For His Children
1.Family 2.Children 3.Men

Printed in the United States of America

ISBN: 0-9653274-2-6

To obtain information regarding an internet service that will protect
your family call American Family Online @ 1-888-817-9314

The song "Wednesday's Prayer" appears on the CD "At The Potter's House"
by Steve and Annie Chapman.
Order from S&A Family, Inc. • P.O. Box 535 • Madison, TN 37116.

Wednesday's Prayer

Contents

This book is dedicated to the two
people in my life who have caused me
more prayer than anyone else in the world,
Nathan and Heidi,
my children.

WEDNESDAY'S PRAYER

Father God to You I come
In the name of Your Son
I bring my children to Your throne
Father hear my cry

Above all else, Lord, save their souls
Draw them near You keep them close
Be the shield against their foes
Make them Yours not mine

Give them peace in Christ alone
In their sorrow be their song
No other joy would last as long
Father calm their fear

Guide their feet, Lord, light their path
May their eyes on You be cast
Give their hands a kingdom task
A purpose for their years

And as my flesh cries out for bread
May I hunger, Lord, instead
That my children would be fed
On Your words of life

So...Father God to You I come
In the name of Your Son
I bring my children to Your throne
Father hear my cry

Steve Chapman / Times & Seasons Music / BMI / 1998

Introduction

The evening was to be an enjoyable time of reconnecting with some friends at a local restaurant. When we gathered in the waiting area, Annie and I knew immediately that something wasn't right. There was a tension in the air between the couple as we made small talk.

As our meal was disappearing and our time together faded, the urgency we felt in asking if things were "O.K." with them bore down on us. Finally, Annie went to the bottom line.

"How are you two doing?"

That question forced the door open to some serious conversation that lasted nearly until closing time. Annie and I tipped the waiter very well for the extra time we spent in the booth with our precious and hurting friends.

We discovered that their teen-age daughter was "giving them fits." Rebellion and "hanging" with some young people who had questionable moral standards caused this couple to feel that their child was slipping away into the abyss of hopelessness.

Annie, who is incredibly perceptive, asked, "How is this effecting the two of you?" The wife responded with an alarming answer. "We can't stand each other! Every time we look at one another we see only blame for the condition our daughter is in. Something has to change. Otherwise, this family is going to completely fall apart!"

Our hearts were moved by their desperate cry for comfort and encouragement. We knew their marriage was first on the list of things that needed healing...and rightly so. They agreed to make it a priority to seek counsel regarding their relationship. But as much as their marriage needed attention, I felt a gnawing need to address their daughter's situation.

The dad was at a loss about how to reach his first born of three kids. Too many arrivals back at home after midnight and far too many of her friends leading her into unacceptable types of entertainment had sapped his strength and willingness to think about his wife. With that knowledge, I decided that the "tyranny of the urgent" dictated that the dad and I go to God on the girl's behalf. The course she was on was too deadly to ignore. That's when I was impressed to make the dad an offer. "Let's begin praying in earnest for your daughter," I said, "and to show God that we're serious about this, I am willing to fast at least once a week with you on her behalf!" Little did I know that just a few days prior, the Lord had impressed on his heart to add fasting to his prayers for his child. Though he had never faced that type of challenge, he was confident that God was leading him to do so. So without hesitation, he enthusiastically responded,

"Let's do it. I really do want to see God do a mighty work in my daughter."

The mother sort of laughed at the idea of us fasting for all of our kids. I don't believe her reaction to our plan was malicious. Instead, I am convinced that it indicated just how deep she had fallen into her own hopelessness. In spite of her discouraging outlook, we set out to reclaim a teen-ager.

That night the dad and I agreed that Wednesdays seemed to be the best day for both of us. It was mid-week and church night, as well as the least busy in our work schedules. Thus began a journey for the two of us that has lasted for several years.

Nearly half a decade has gone by and the report we can give is glorious. The daughter has passed by hell. Slowly, she began to show signs of spiritual recovery. Gradually her friends began to change and the influence of godly company replaced the "bad company" that had corrupted good morals. Today, she is totally different.

One of the sweetest moments I have ever experienced in a church service was on an Easter Sunday about three years after my friend and I started "doing Wednesdays" together. Annie and I had taken our seats in the balcony of the church and about six or seven rows below us was the couple we had grown to love so much. As the worship music filled the room, Annie nudged me and quietly pointed toward our friends. What I saw filled my heart with indescribable joy. Standing next to her dad was the daughter who had been the object of many a Wednesday past. The memory of hunger pains faded far into the distance as I saw her lift her hands and her eyes in praise to our Father in heaven who had heard our prayers. What a beautiful sight it was!

Admittedly, it was an emotional roller coaster ride through the years invested in our quest for her soul. We had to face some facts. One, the daughter, like all the rest of us, was born with a sinful nature and because of it, she was prone to sin (Romans 3:23/7:18). Two, "as the serpent deceived Eve by his craftiness..." (II Corinthians 11:3) Satan was ready at all times to target her weaknesses. Ultimately, we realized that our struggle was not against flesh and blood, but against the unseen forces that sought to deceive her (Ephesians 6:12). Yet, a confidence in the Lord's ability to overcome the "god of this world" remained. Also, the accountability to one another as men was helpful. We occasionally "checked up" on our commitment to our routine of prayer when we met at church or at the woods to go hunting. Not much was said other than, "Still doin' Wednesdays?" The answer was always a smile and a determined, "Yep!"

The thing that seemed to encourage us the most was seeing the little changes in the daughter, or hearing sweet words that she had not said in a long while. These indications that she was "coming home to Christ" did more to spur us on than nearly anything. Watching God at work was a spiritual delight. Add to that the dad's absolute and unconditional love for his teen-ager and the result was glorious. Though the outcome has been extremely gratifying to us both, we have not abandoned our custom. In fact, we have agreed that it is more important now than ever before that we continue in our prayers and fasting for our kids. Satan does not cease his pursuit of our children, neither should we let up in the battle. So the Wednesday's prayer goes on...and will hopefully persist until our last day on earth.

Perhaps at this time in your role as father you see the need to "get serious" in your prayers for your kids. Maybe your child is yet to be born, or you're the dad of a babe in arms. Possibly your kids are toddlers or teen-agers. Or, perhaps your children are grown and out of the "the nest." At whatever stage of fatherhood you might be, if you are concerned for the spiritual destination of your children and want to establish a regimen of prayer and fasting for them, the following pages are for you.

This book is a non-exhaustive, quick read, designed to simply "jump-start" you on the rewarding journey you will make on the knees of your heart. As you go may God abundantly give you wisdom to know more about His great ability and willingness to hear your cries on behalf of your children.

Why We Must Pray

I believe my sanity, safety, and even the salvation of my soul is an answer to the prayers of my parents. I was born in 1950, three years after my folks were married in 1947. Soon after they vowed to a life together, and before the kids came along, my mother, who had experienced a "walk on the wild side of life," was radically converted at a local revival near the town of Chapmanville, West Virginia. God used her salvation experience to eventually influence my dad to his own decision to become a Christian. Then came my sister and me.

I have no recollection of not being in a "churched" family. Rarely did we miss darkening the doors of our neighborhood sanctuary. We were beyond regular attendees, we were fixtures in the pews. My dad ultimately responded to a call on his life to become a preacher and took a pastor's position in the town of Point Pleasant, West Virginia, along the Ohio River.

When my sister and I had reached our teen years, we were essentially the music program at our church. My mother had taught me to play the guitar and by mimicking the piano style of the late, great instrumentalist, Floyd Cramer, I had developed some limited skill on the keyboard. (I was known to play one of his songs, "Last Date," during altar services...at least until someone recognized the melody!) Jeannie, my sister, and I were vital parts of our parent's ministry.

However, as the enemy of our souls will inevitably do, he made a play for the Chapman kids. In my early teens I began to slide down the slippery slope of the world's enticements. It was in that era of time that my mother shocked me one morning with a prayer I shall never forget.

I was laying in bed around 8 a.m. when she came bursting into my room. As I attempted to arouse myself from a sleepy stupor, she dropped to her knees and grabbed my right forearm. The words I heard next are in the chorus of the following song I wrote about the incident a few years later. I affectionately call it, "Mama's Brave Prayer." You must keep in mind as you read this lyric that I had watched my mother's prayers be answered sometimes within minutes. She had a connection with God that was nothing less than intimidating. And it was this sweet, humble woman...my mother... who did the following to me:

MAMA'S BRAVE PRAYER

One day in my early teen-age years
Mama came into my room with tears
She said, "I've put it off too long

What I've got to do seems wrong."
Next to my bed she fell on her knees
She laid her hard workin' hands on me
Looked up to Jesus and told Him she cared
That's when I heard my Mama's brave prayer.

"If you see he'll die a sinner
If you see he'll trade the right for the wrong
Then all I ask of you, sweet Jesus,
Go ahead, right now, and take him on home!"

She said, "Amen," and the room grew still
I'll not forget the fear I could feel
And the moments passed
So have the years
And I'm glad to say that I'm still here
Now lookin' back I can see it's true
She loved my flesh and my spirit too.
Now Heaven waits us and I believe I'll be there
And I'll be forever grateful for my Mama's
     brave prayer.

"If you see he'll die a sinner
If you see he'll trade the right for the wrong
Then all I ask of you sweet Jesus
Go ahead, right now
And take him on home!"

(Steve Chapman / Times and Seasons Music / BMI)
From the CD, "The Silver Bridge"/ Steve Chapman

Needless to say, that morning is the day I learned what "cold sweat" was all about. I honestly thought my life was going to come to a screeching halt after my mother finished her cry to heaven. But like the lyric says, "I'm glad I'm still here!"

So why would anyone offer a prayer like my mother's? My answer is—we pray because the worst thing that could ever happen to our children is not that they would flunk out of school, marry a jerk, or even fall prey to a deadly disease. While those things are indeed awful to consider, the very worst thing that could ever befall our children is that they would die without Christ in their hearts and as a result, suffer the consequences of the eternal and unquenchable flames of hell, forever separated from God and those who love them. (see Mark 9:48) That's why we fall on our knees for them! Please consider this lyric:

Daddy Dip Your Finger In The Water

I had a dream and it seemed so real
I can't explain the sadness I could feel
I heard my child cryin' somewhere in the dark
And what I heard, Lord it broke my heart

"Daddy, dip your finger in the water
Come and touch my tongue
These flames around me are gettin' hotter
And I have nowhere to run
Come and touch my tongue!"

I ran to the voice and I came to the edge
Of a canyon deep and I stood on the ledge
And far below me where the darkness never ends
I heard my child cryin' out again

"Daddy dip your finger in the water
Come and touch my tongue
These flames around me are gettin' hotter
And I have nowhere to run
Come and touch my tongue!"

I knew between us was a great divide
I could not cross to the other side
And as I fell down on my knees
I heard my child say these words to me.

"Daddy, tell my sisters and my brothers
This truth we somehow missed
Jesus is the way there is no Other
Who can save a soul from a place like this..."

"Oh! Daddy, dip your finger in the water
Come and touch my tongue
These flames around me are gettin' hotter
And I have nowhere to run
Come and touch my tongue!
Just come and touch my tongue!"

(Steve Chapman / Times and Seasons Music / BMI)
From the CD, "At The Potter's House" / Steve and Annie Chapman

Surely none of us want this to be the outcome of our children's lives. And, far be it from any of us who are fathers that we would be guilty of ignoring our son's and daughter's great need for knowing Christ. Based on my experience with the prayers of my own parents for me, I do believe that it will take fervent, serious, and persistent prayers to insure that our kids will accept Christ and know His salvation. I am convinced that because of Him, they can pass through time confident in their salvation and filled with joy that is unspeakable. And someday, when time is no more, we will join with them on "the other side" around the throne of God to celebrate His deliverance through the "Red Seas" of life.

Why Add Fasting To Our Prayers?

It is likely that you have driven slowly by a serious car wreck on the highway and felt that squeamish feeling. Do you remember how it stayed with you, haunted you, and caused you to drive very carefully for the next several miles? Then at some point down the road the memory of the tragedy fades into the distance. The next thing you know your "rpm's" are in the red range again. That's a vivid picture of my teen years as they passed after my "Mama's Brave Prayer." It shook me for a long time. Then, as I entered my late teens and journeyed on into my early 20's, enough years had gone by that I felt comfortable about putting aside godly fear and began to think of those "pleasures of life" that I had not been allowed to experience.

By then I had decided to postpone college and I joined the U.S. Navy. Unlike my time at a nearby university where I was still physically close to family and friends, I was practically alone in the military. It was a tempting environment for untried sin which, I sadly admit, I chose not to resist.

I was moved around to the big cities of Chicago, Memphis, and Norfolk, Virginia. It was in these places, out of the eyesight of those who loved me and held me accountable to a good moral standard, that I chose to "carry out the desires of the flesh" (Galatians 5:16) One wise gentleman said, "Character is what you are when there ain't nobody lookin'!" That is a truth I mocked during my military days.

I was on my way to becoming that "spiritual wreck" that others would drive by and feel squeamish at the sight of it. I had entered what I called, "my dark ages." While it was sadly true that the enemy had only escalated his battle tactics that were aimed at my destruction, my folks had also kicked things into high gear in terms of their prayerful determination to see their kid in heaven. They were very familiar with the words of I Peter 5:8. "Be of sober spirit, be on the alert. Your adversary, the devil, prowls about like a roaring lion, seeking someone to devour." They were not about to let the enemy win nor intimidate them with his toothless growls. Their hunger to see their son return to the safety of a walk with Christ consumed them.

My folks embraced II Corinthians 10:3, 4 as truth. "For though we walk in the flesh, we do not war according to the flesh, for the weapons of our warfare are not of the flesh, but divinely powerful for the destruction of fortresses." They knew that the fight would be won only with God's help. Having no where else to turn but to the Lord, they poured their hearts into praying for me and bravely, they became acquainted with hunger.

Fasting has a side effect that actually aids a person in their prayers. When that gnawing in the belly of the flesh begins to get one's attention, it can be like the proverbial "string around the finger" that is a reminder to pray. That tinge of hunger is the tug on the hem of God's garment...so to speak. The eyes of flesh are better able to see the eternal purpose of prayer when they are focused on heaven and not on the pot on the stove.

Also, fasting seems to help open one's spiritual eyes to the battle that rages in "the other world," which flesh and blood cannot touch. I am personally familiar with the higher degree of spiritual insight that a parent can gain when they have replaced eating with the eternal welfare of a child. I came face to face with this type of supernatural understanding when, once again, God used my mother to rescue my life from the stronghold of Satan's death grip. I was re-captured, believe it or not, on another morning, eight years later, in the same bedroom where she had prayed that "brave prayer" over me when I was thirteen. By then, I was in my early twenties and dabbling in drugs as a sailor in the Navy.

I had come home one weekend on a three day leave from Norfolk, Virginia to visit my folks and found that they were gone, attending a church convention several miles away. Their absence left me alone in the house. In the solitude of the kitchen, I took out my pipe, put the windows up, and proceeded to smoke some dope. The drug induced paranoia was severe and began to ravage my mind. I got really nervous about the possibility that my folks would return unexpectedly and "catch me in my sin." Though I knew what I was doing was wrong and I feared devastating my folks with the knowledge of my involvement in drugs, I continued in my foolishness. Before putting my pipe away, I cleaned it using the fuzzy, white, flexible wires designed for the job. As I sat trance-like in the kitchen, I looked at the evidence of my wrong-doing scattered on the table, and I decided I needed to carefully hide the half dozen, brown stained cleaners.

First I wadded them up in a tiny ball and wrapped them in a paper napkin. Then I ripped the lid off of a Campbell's Soup can that was empty and stuffed them into the bottom of the can. After that, I opened the mouth of an empty, half-gallon, waxed milk carton and crammed the soup can containing the pipe cleaners into the bottom. Then I took all the trash out of the waste basket under the sink and put that milk carton in the very bottom, put the trash back on top, and shoved it confidently back under the sink.

Two weeks later I went home again to see my family for the weekend. Sunday morning came and once more, it was time for me to head back to Virginia. Before I got up, my mother softly came in and sat down next to me on the edge of the bed. She said, "Son, are you going to go to church with us this morning before you leave for the ship?" I wanted her to hear my resistance to the idea, so I answered with a half-hearted, "Oh...I guess I will."

Then, with a slight waver in her voice that always told me something significant was about to be heard, she asked, "Son, whose pipe cleaners were those in the trash can?" I'm convinced that was a question that originated in heaven but reverberated in the halls of hell. The enemy's camp was aroused. And for sure, so was my attention!

I was in total shock. I had no time to prepare a defense. I was caught "red-handed" and had no other choice than to confess my sin. She cried, I cried, all God's children cried in the Chapman household. I was almost relieved in a way. There would be no more need to hide behind my wall of fleshly virtue that I had learned to display when around my loved ones.

Eventually, I came to see that it was God's mercy that had allowed my mother's spiritual eyes to be opened to my transgression. It was His love and grace that had granted me the opportunity to let Him deal with my sin within the walls of time instead of at the judgment that will follow my appointment with death (Hebrews 9:27). I repented and changed directions. I was also deeply grateful when my folks assured me that while they could never condone my actions, they loved me because I belonged to them. That day I learned what unconditional love truly meant.

In light of the fact that Satan is so subtle, plus the fact that our children are bent toward sinning, you can see why I believe in adding fasting to our prayers for our kids. I want to see them in heaven, and I desire for the Lord to take me serious when I take them to His throne in prayer.

Maybe you are seeking the Lord about a child who is yet to surrender to Christ. As you pray for them to come to know His forgiveness, may God make you mighty in the Spirit, and strengthen you as you face the pains of hunger.

Perhaps you are thinking of a child who is danger-ously teetering on the brink of spiritual oblivion. If this is true, may I encourage you to join the army of those who are praying for their children. Let God see your invisible hunger for their salvation by pushing away the visible plate for a while. While you pray for your chil-dren, remember the Psalmist David's words, "Blessed be the Lord, because he has heard the voice of my supplica-tions" (Psalm 28:6). May they help you to trust the Lord for the results. It might take some time, but don't give up in the battle. A little while here on earth is no compari-son to the unending expanse of eternity. I hope you will be encouraged by the lyric that follows. As you read it, please understand that no matter how distant your child is from God, there is hope. Consider the widow of Nain in Luke 7:11-17 who had brought her only son to Jesus. The boy was dead. Yet, Jesus had compassion on the mother and told her, "Do not weep." Then He touched the coffin and spoke to the son. "Young man, I say to you, arise!" And the dead man arose and began to speak.

After that, Jesus gave him back to his mother. What a beautiful picture of what we must do for our sons and daughters who are spiritually dead in their trespasses and sins" (Ephesians 1:1-5). We must take them to Jesus, for He alone can make them "alive" again! Please be encouraged because your child is...

REACHABLE

There's a boy in his mother's prayers
Cause lately she's been aware
That he's been drifting too far from the shore
And she's beginning to believe
The boy is getting out of reach
Weary mother, don't you worry anymore.

Cause...
The boy is reachable
Oh he's reachable
And to God he's visible
And all things are possible
Cause if the Lord can reach His hand of love
    through time
And touch a cold sinner's heart like mine
The boy is reachable
I know he's reachable.

And there's a girl
On her daddy's heart

Cause lately they've drifted apart
And the company she's keeping
Leads her further away
And he's beginning to believe
The girl is getting out of reach
Oh, weary father
Heaven hears you when you pray

And the girl is reachable
I know she's reachable
And to God she's visible
And all things are possible
Cause if the Lord can reach his hand
    of love through time
And touch a cold sinner's heart like mine
The girl is reachable
I know she's reachable.

(Steve Chapman / Times and Seasons Music / BMI)
From the CD, "Family Favorites" / Steve and Annie Chapman

The First Step

"I have no greater joy than this, to hear of my children walking in the truth." These words, found in III John 4, were, of couse, referring to spiritual children. But, when applied to the role of the parent, the sentiment is the same. Proverbs 23:15 also speaks well for the parent whose child is walking with God. "My son if your heart is wise, my own heart will also be glad; and my inmost being will rejoice; when your lips speak what is right." It is true that a deep and glorious joy fills a father's heart when their son or daughter chooses to follow Christ. It is an indescribable gladness that wells up inside when I see my children choosing God's way instead of the way of the world. I know when they set their eyes on the "things above," and not the vanity of that which is below, they will find true and lasting joy in all their days.

If it is true that so great a joy is found in a child choosing to follow Christ, then would it not be fair to say that a great sorrow comes when we see them reject the walk in truth? In Luke, the 11th chapter, you'll find the account of the prodigal son. Imagine, if you will, what anguish his father must have felt when he would think of his wayward child. I can almost see him crying as the waves of sadness rushed onto the shores of his heart. The first verse and chorus of the song, *Turn Your Heart Toward Home*, attempts to describe what the scene might have looked like in the home of that hurting dad:

Late in the evening
When everyone was sleeping
The father of the wayward son
Slipped out in the night
He looked toward the city
And wiped away the tears
And prayed his son
Could hear his father's cry

"Turn your heart toward home
Turn your heart toward home
You've been gone so long
Turn your heart toward home."

(S. Chapman / Dawn Treader Music / SESAC)
From the CD, "At The Potter's House" / Steve and Annie Chapman

Oh! How that dad must have prayed for his lost son. In the same way that I believe it was the result of the prayers of my parents that brought about my return, I consider it likely that it was God's answer to that father's earnest supplications that caused the young man to suddenly come to his senses in the pig-pen and begin his journey homeward. Someday, when I meet that well known prodigal in heaven, we can rejoice together in thanks to God for parents who "went to the mat" for us.

The soldier fathers who are fighting for their children on the front lines of prayer have responded to a call issued to their hearts by the Heavenly Father, a summons which they consider to be extremely urgent. With a sense of alarm, these men have awakened to the fact that there is no time to waste in reclaiming a child for the Lord. One dad said, "Until I saw the emergency, I didn't feel the urgency!"

Sadly, however, too many fathers are slumbering in their spiritual recliners, oblivious to the deadly serpent that has slithered into their home, and ultimately into the hearts of their children. The venomous viper is clever in his ability to find his way into our lives. He rarely comes crashing through the front door of the home. That tactic would get too much immediate attention. He is much more shrewd. He looks for less obvious ways to get in such as bickering, unforgiveness, and even a bitterness that may be seething in a family member.

Unfortunately, the breach in the fort around the family through which the enemy passes is often found in the hearts of dads. Sometimes, without ever knowing it, a father can create a crack in the wall of the home with things that seem innocent on the surface. However, upon closer examination, that which seems harmless is really the tool that Satan uses like a crowbar to pry open an entry into the home. A prime example of that type of opening is the entertainment a dad allows and endorses. Permitting a steady diet of the brain- numbing nonsense that comes through network television, cable channels, low standard movie rentals, certain books, and maga- zines can slowly chisel away at the hearts of the family members. Most of Hollywood is not just an entertain- ment source, it is a machine designed to reshape and remold the minds and hearts of its captives. And so often, what we dads consider mild and acceptable in terms of content is ultimately the bait that is used by the destroyer to entice our kids to the trap of the more sor- didly immoral material. One wise observer noted, "What parents accept in moderation, the children will embrace in excess!" How sobering a thought. And how true!

Far worse than what the whole family might devour in terms of worthless entertainment is what the dad may consume in secret. And in many cases, he does so with the foolish assumption that it affects no one else, includ- ing his kids. To the contrary, whatever a dad does, whether openly or in secret, will eventually have a bear- ing on the lives of his children. Consider the truth in Lamentations 5:7. "Our fathers sinned and are no more; it is we who have borne their iniquities." It is an undeni- able reality that a dad's transgression will have a negative effect on the life of a child. This truth was never meant to be a license for a son or daughter to engage in sinful con- duct, instead, it is to be taken by the fathers as a stern warning, "... be sure your sins will find you out," and "...Do not be deceived, God is not mocked; for whatever a man sows, this he will also reap." (Numbers 32:23 & Galatians 6:7)

I heard from some friends of ours (whom I will call Bill and Sheri) about the desperate call they received one evening from a mom. She begged them to come as quickly as they could. Our friends hurried to the home and when they arrived, the dad was in an uncontrolled frenzy. Bill and Sheri quickly learned that the son had a pregnant girlfriend and the mother feared that her husband's intense anger would lead to actions that would do more harm than good.

During the evening, a necessary lull in the heated conversation took place and while they broke for a few minutes to allow the frazzled mom and dad to quickly tend to another matter, Sheri sat down at the family's personal computer. With permission to do so, she began to "toy" with the PC. Within moments a devastating discovery was made. Sheri, who happened to be a "wiz" with the operation of a computer, punched a few buttons and the screen revealed that someone had been accessing several Internet sites that featured the lowest grades of pornography. Sheri brought the couple's attention to what she had found. She did so assuming that it was the son who had been the one dabbling in the raunchy material. The mother quickly called her boy into the room and confronted him about the matter. With an expression of horror, he said nothing then looked at his dad with stark fear. The father stood quietly by, but the look on his face was that of total shock. Suddenly, the sickening truth fell on everyone in the room. The dad was the guilty party. When all eyes turned to him, he initially claimed innocence. Suddenly, he realized that there was no way out of the corner he was in and he began to weep. With a stream of tears running down his face, he admitted that in the deep of the night he had been secretly "surfing the net," indulging in the sin that had so easily captured his mind. He had no idea that another pair of eyes was watching and that an unintentional consent to feed a youthful lust was given to his son. The poison of pornography had not only corrupted the dad, it had devastated his boy's young life.

Bill and Sheri pointed to the father's indulgence as the route by which Satan had gotten to their teen-ager. They prayed with the family and encouraged the dad to "close the breach" by repenting of his sin, ceasing his visits to the web traps, and allowing himself to be accountable to his family in terms of his lustful nature.

That dad's story is a sobering example of the first step we fathers must take in praying for our kids. We should allow God to purify our hearts, be "transformed by the renewing of your mind, (Romans 12:1,2), and we must take "every thought captive to the obedience of Christ." (I Corinthians 10:5) Whether its the garbage heap of entertainment or any other transgression, we cannot ignore the long term damaging effects of sin. Think carefully about the admonition found in Isaiah 59:2. "But your iniquities have made a separation between you and your God, And your sins hid His face from you, so that He does not hear."

How can we ever see the critical needs of our children if our spiritual eyes cannot see over the wall of our own sin? And how can we be heard in heaven when our prayers are hitting the soundproof barrier of our iniquities? May we wake up and climb out of our easy chairs, fall on our knees, and let God cleanse us and prepare us to do battle for the souls of our precious children.

THE SECRET PLACE

My heart is like a house
One day I let the Savior in
And there are many rooms
Where we would visit now and then
But then one day He saw that door
I knew the day had come too soon
I said Jesus I'm not ready
For us to visit in that room.

Cause that's a place in my heart
Where even I don't go
I have some things hidden there
I don't want no one to know
But He handed me the keys

With tears of love on His face
He said I want to make you clean
Let me go in your secret place

So I opened up the door
And as the two of us walked in
I was so ashamed
His light revealed my hidden sin
But when I think about that room now
I'm not afraid anymore
Cause I know my hidden sin
No longer hides behind that door

That was a place in my heart
Where even I wouldn't go
I had some things hidden there
I didn't want no one to know
But he handed me the keys
With tears of love on his face
He made me clean
I let Him in my secret place.

(Steve Chapman / Careers-BMG Music Pub./ Shepherd's Fold Music/
Star Song)
From the CD, "Family Favorites"/ Steve and Annie Chapman

How and When

As the concern for the salvation of your children grows daily in your heart, and you face the increasing reality of the literal lake of fire that they can avoid by trusting in Christ alone (see Revelation 21:8), you will want to do more than just pray casual and occasional sentence prayers for them. You will want to cry out to God for your kid's sake. And, it is possible that you now see the desperate need to defy the flesh for the sake of this spiritual cause. If that is true, there is no better way to accomplish that than fasting.

Many of us wince at the idea of missing a meal. Our love for a good "gastronomical jubilee" is enormous. The very thought of passing up any opportunity to feed our appetites is depressing enough to make us run out and grab a Twinkie to console our threatened taste buds.

There's nothing wrong with food, of course. God, in His wisdom, put the yearning for it in our system. Then, He supplied the resources for growing and harvesting that which would fuel our bodies. Food not only meets a biological need, but it also helps fill the emotional need for companionship as we converse across the table at dinner time. "Breaking bread" together has been a symbol of friendship since man has walked the earth. We need food for many reasons.

If man's need for food is so great, why then, would God see our forsaking of it as an honorable sacrifice? Could it be that through the discipline of closing our mouths to food, we open our hearts to Him? When you consider Nehemiah's response to hearing about the great distress of the Jewish exiles, you can see that fasting is indeed a fleshly display of an intense hunger to be heard by the Lord (Nehemiah 1:4, 5).

I should add that going without food is, by no means, a replacement for the finished work of Christ. There is no dispensing of saving grace through any of our human efforts. "For by grace you have been saved through faith; and that not of yourselves, it is the gift of God; not as a result of works, that no one should boast." (Ephesians 2:9)

Also, nothing human should ever get the glory for what is accomplished by the hand of God. "Not to us, O Lord, not to us, but to Thy name give glory because of Thy lovingkindness, because of Thy truth." (Psalm 115:1) Any impressive results from our simple sacrifice in the form of fasting and prayer should never be to serve our egos. Instead, may we humbly say, "May God be praised!"

With that in mind, if you are ready to take the first step in the extra mile that fasting adds to your prayers for your children, then brace yourself for an exciting journey. As you begin this walk of sacrificial love for your kids, keep in mind the fact that your flesh will constantly resist the idea. You will find that you are capable of coming up with some of the lamest excuses imaginable to avoid the process. From, "I have a headache," to "I need the energy for my aerobics class," your resolve will be tested. And, it's likely that you'll succumb at times. Still your determination to stick with the regimen must be driven by a greater need than the one your belly screams about!

It's hard to understand it, but some parents of troubled kids are ready and willing to take out second mortgages to get a child into a re-hab center. They would sell all they have to invest in expert counselors while all along ignoring the available effectiveness of consistently taking their kids to the altar and hungrily presenting them to God. The invitation to begin doing just that, if you haven't started already, is extended even at this moment. Shall we pray...and fast!

The following are my recommendations regarding the challenge of adding a fast to your prayers. In no way am I implying that these suggestions are the best and only techniques. The fact is, there is no set method for prayer and fasting. While there are biblical precedents such as Jesus' forty day fast (Matthew 4) and "Daniel's fast" (Daniel 1:8-13), the sacrifice you make for your kids should be done according to your conviction and a wise assessment of your circumstances.

A person, for example, with a known medical problem that would preclude them from changing their dietary habits, should first consult a physician. In that case, going without specific foods such as sweets or caffeine, or even sacrificing other delights such as entertainment, would be a worthy alternative. For those who are sure that fasting would not present a health risk, then food is definitely first on the list of the things to forsake. Whether your fasting is restricted to non-food items or you are able to forego the "tasty morsels," don't forget that the purpose of the fast is to remind us to humbly demonstrate the seriousness of your requests before the Almighty, and to admit that your kids are far more important than your own gratification!

As for choosing when to fast, that too should be a personal decision. At first, I chose to begin at 8 a.m. on Wednesdays. I quickly realized that I was capable of "making it too easy" by being sure to eat a hardy breakfast prior to starting time. Wanting more out of the experience I decided to start the fast at bed time the night before. Many times, it is tempting to stuff myself before I retire on Tuesday night in order to avoid the Wednesday "growls." I know to do so, however, would be defeating the purpose. The thing I look for, and sincerely need on Wednesdays, is that sharp hunger pain in the gut about mid-day to remind me of my kids. It simply will not happen if my stomach is still full from the previous evening's four course picnic I consumed.

I also discovered that it was very easy to forget my commitment to Wednesday's prayer and fasting. Several times I would bound out of bed, grab a granola bar and coffee, and head off down the road in my pick-up, sipping and eating as I drove! Suddenly, a few miles and burps down the highway, I would realize what I had done and feel terrible. In that case I would set my sights on Thursday.

In this quest for a serious prayer regimen-**flexibility** is a must. Sometimes a luncheon falls on Wednesday or family arrives unexpectedly at noon from a far away city. When circumstances such as these are beyond my control and it changes my strategy, I know its time to make new plans. If I know in advance that Wednesday will be blocked, I opt for Tuesday, a day earlier. Sometimes, spreading the process over a two day period (fasting until noon both days) is necessary. However its done, denying the flesh for a season in order to attain a spiritual goal sometimes requires a willingness to accommodate the rest of the world around us. Oddly enough, once a dad begins to see the encouraging results in the children that fasting brings about, it may cause a firm resistance to revising the schedule. Still, adaptability will be a valuable virtue. (Of course, if fasting becomes impossible during a particular week, by all means, don't forget to pray.)

When to break your fast is also a personal choice. For

me, ending at 4 p.m. seemed to be the best time because my family usually eats our evening meal somewhat early. On some occasions, if I want to extend my abstinence from food for a little longer at the end of the day, I feel free to do so as long as Annie knows in advance. Though changes in your schedule will occur, I suggest that you pick a time to pray and fast and make it as regular as possible. This is a courtesy for the sake of the family's schedule as well as the person who may be preparing a meal.

Finally, speaking from experience, you must keep in mind that all of us have two enemies. The flesh and Satan. Both will not want you to see victory in praying and fasting for your kids. Your fallen, sinful nature will be tempted to tout the fact that you are going without food. To do so will only weaken your weapon. Instead of heralding the fact, be careful to follow the instructions given in Matthew 6:16-18. "And whenever you fast, do not put on a gloomy face as the hypocrites do, for they neglect their appearance in order to be seen fasting by men. Truly I say to you, they have their reward in full. But you, when you fast, anoint your head, and wash your face so that you may not be seen fasting by men, but by your Father who is in secret; and your Father who sees in secret will repay you." If a period of fasting is done well, only your family will know about it. What is done privately will be rewarded openly. And in this case, the reward will show in the lives of your children.

Our other enemy, Satan, will try to deceive you with a

"guilt trip" if you fail even one time to follow through with your commitment. He'll want you to grovel in remorse and waste your energy. Even your salvation may be the target of the doubt he will try to sow in your heart. Instead of falling prey to his tactics, enlist the 32ND Psalm of David, verse 5. "I acknowledged my sin to Thee, and my iniquity I did not hide; I said, 'I will confess my transgression to the Lord'; and Thou didst forgive the guilt of my sin." With your hope only in Christ, continue on with a determination to not squander another opportunity to bless your children by taking them to the Throne of God with prayer and fasting.

What Shall Be Said

You may be wondering, "How can I pray for my kids while I go about my daily business?" Or, "Should I kneel or bow my head while I'm at work?" "How can Wednesdays, or whatever day I chose, be devoted to praying if I'm obligated to perform a job?"

These are legitimate concerns. By no means would I suggest that a boss be cheated out of his time while you pray for your children. The wise thing to do instead, is to be a "weaver," threading your prayers through the holes of time that come available to you throughout the day. On your way to work, for example, turn off the radio and pray. During a break at your job, take a walk (if you can) and pray. During a lunch hour, when it will be extra difficult to conceal your fast, find a quiet corner and read the scriptures. The re-enforcement that an encouraging passage can offer will be timely. On the trip home, instead of singing along with "Garth" or "Celine," turn them off and make your own music by singing your prayers for your kids out loud to the Lord (if you are alone in the car, of course!). Generally, devote the free moments of your schedule to the interest of your children. It may seem fragmented and insignificant at times but be assured, the accumulation of your efforts will not go unseen!

During the day there will likely be stretches of time when you cannot verbalize a prayer. The beauty of fasting is that even though you may not be lifting your voice aloud to the Lord, your attitude of devotion is noticed in heaven. The silent cry of praying that God hears takes place in those moments when you feel the "bumps of hunger" in the road on your way to supper. Rejoice in the pain because the purpose for which you sacrifice and pray is frequently brought back to your attention. Fasting fills the gaps!

And now, what shall be said when you do pray? I suggest, first of all, that you decide on two or three desires that you have for your kids and make them a part of your prayers each week or every time you go to the Lord on their behalf. It is not a bother to God to approach Him with an ongoing request. In Luke 18:1-7 we find this comforting account:

Now He was telling them a parable to show that at all times they ought to pray and not to lose heart, saying, "There was in a certain city a judge who did not fear God, and did not respect man. And there was a widow in that city, and she kept coming to him saying, 'Give me legal protection from my opponent.' And for a while he was unwilling; but afterward he said to himself, 'Even though I do not fear God nor respect man, yet because this widow bothers me, I will give her legal protection, lest by continually coming she wear me out.' (My margin says, "hit me under the eye!") And the Lord said, 'Hear what the unrighteous judge said; now shall not God bring about justice for His elect, who cry to Him day and night, and will He delay long over them?'"

The widow in this passage was commended for her persistence. As a result of her unwavering petitions, her request was granted. Don't be backward about doing the same for your kids. Too many times we actually feel that we are "pestering" God with our repeated prayers. Instead, He takes delight in them.

There are two requests that I settled on for Nathan and Heidi that I have made a part of every Wednesday's prayer—that they would have *peace* and *purpose*. First, the peace I desire for them is found only in knowing and following Jesus Christ. Second, that He would grant them a purpose in His kingdom here on earth. I am confident that if these two things are true for them, they will be people who are content, disciplined, and valuable to their community and their nation. Several times through the day on Wednesdays, and throughout the week or whenever they come to mind, I will utter these simple words, "God give them peace and purpose!"

I also include other requests that are often dictated by

whatever they may be going through at the time. Tests at school, a problem with a friend, safety on the highway, or a choice regarding a social event are the types of needs they may be facing. And in the future when they are "out of the nest," perhaps with their own families, I will continue to keep my ear tuned to their needs. There are as many things to pray about as there are children to pray for. I guarantee that you will not be lost for subjects when it comes to praying for your kids.

If this process of prayer is new to you, the following pages contain a breakdown of the lyrics to the song, "Wednesday's Prayer." Feel free to use these words as a guide to helping you get started down this glorious path of prayer. As you proceed, I'm sure you will add your own phrases to the lyric.

In closing, I suggest that you write a special note to your child (or children) telling them of your plan to pray. Believe me, whether they show it or not, they'll be grateful for such a display of your love. Your note might read:

"Dear (child's name), As your dad, I am committing to pray and fast for you on (the day you choose) of each week. I love you and I know our Heavenly Father loves you too. We both care! Please let me know if you have any specific needs you want me to include when I take you to God's throne in prayer. From my heart, Dad.

At the end of this book you will find a section called "Room to Write." This is for your convenience in writing down your ongoing prayers, as well as recording the outcome. This section can be carefully preserved and passed on to them in years to come.

Also included is a word of wisdom from Annie for the moms who look forward to facilitating a dad's decision to establish a regular regimen of prayer and fasting for their kids. And along with her words, she relates how Nathan and Heidi feels about being the object of so many Wednesday's Prayers.

May God richly bless you and your family as you embark on this marvelous journey.

"Father God, to you I come..."

You are my "Father who art in heaven."
I am one of the fathers "who aren't in heaven."
Thank You for letting me belong to You through
Jesus Christ, Your only begotten Son.
I have no one else to turn to with these
burdens of my heart.

"Casting all your anxiety upon Him,
because He cares for you."
I PETER 5:7

"In the name of your Son..."

I know that it is only through Your
Son, Jesus Christ, that I can
enter into your presence. Thank You
for providing me access to Your
throne.

"I am the way, and the truth, and the
life; no one comes to the Father,
but through me."
John 14:6

"I bring my children to your throne..."

Today I bring to You the children
You have given me,
this bone of my bone, flesh of my flesh.
While I know it is my duty to care for their
earthly needs, in You alone can I put my trust
for their eternal care.

"Behold, children are a gift of the Lord;
The fruit of the womb is a reward.
Like arrows in the hand of a warrior,
So are the children of one's youth."

PSALM 127: 3,4

"Father, hear my cry!"

In my heart, Oh God, I have come to
a sense of urgency
about the spiritual needs of my children.
You alone
know the number of their days.
In this hour, while the walls of time still stand
around us, I lift my
voice to You, that You would give ear
to these things
I am about to ask on their behalf.

"Give ear to my words, O Lord, consider
my groaning.
Heed the sound of my cry for help,
my King and my God,
For to Thee do I pray."

PSALM 5: 1

"Above all else, Lord, save their souls..."

Oh! Lord God,
I know there is not a greater need that
my children have
than for their souls to know the saving grace
that is in
Your Son, Christ Jesus.
May they come quickly to the realization
that He alone
is their only hope for redemption,
and may they call on
Him while He may be found.
Have mercy, O God, on my children!

"And she will bear a Son; and you shall
call His name Jesus, for it is He
who will save His people from their sins."
MATTHEW 1: 21

"Draw them near you, keep them close..."

Daily draw my children to Your side, Oh! Father.
Reveal Yourself to them in very real ways.
When they are tempted with sin,
may Your presence cause
them to choose Your fellowship and not that
of the world.
Put Your eternal arms around them
and help them to
remember whose child they are."

"But Jesus said, Let the children alone,
and do not
hinder them from coming to me."

"I have drawn you with lovingkindness."
MATTHEW 19:14 & JEREMIAH 31: 3

"Be the shield against their foes..."

I have no doubt that the forces of hell
will attempt
to claim my children. Oh! Mighty Father,
protect them
while they sleep and in their waking hours.
And as they journey on this earth,
may You guard their steps.
Oh! Loving Father, keep them from eternal
harm!

"The Lord is my strength and my shield;
My heart trusts in Him, and I am helped..."
PSALM 28: 7

"Make them yours, not mine."

As You gave to us Your Son, Christ Jesus,
I give to You my children. May You cause
the light
of Your love to shine through them
in this dark and sinful world.

"But the angel of the Lord called to him
from heaven,
and said, 'Abraham, Abraham!' And he said,
'Here I am.'
And he said, 'Do not stretch out your hand
against the lad,
and do nothing to harm him; for now
I know that
you fear God, since you have not withheld
your son,
your only son, from Me.'"

GENESIS 22: 11,12

"Give them peace in Christ alone..."

I know that in this world, my children will
experience trials, and pain, and disappointment.
In the midst of their trouble, may the peace
that passes understanding be that which
fills their heart of hearts.

"These things I have spoken to you, that in Me
you may have peace. In the world you have
tribulation, but take courage, I have overcome
the world."

JOHN 16:33

"In their sorrow be their song..."

I know too, that my children will encounter
sadness. As the waves of sorrow wash over their
souls, may You comfort them with Your
gentle presence.

"Because of the multitude of oppressions
they cry out; They cry for help because of
the arm of the mighty,
But no one says, 'Where is God my maker, Who
gives songs in the night...'"
"The Lord is my strength and my song, and He
has become my salvation..."
JOB 35: 9,10 & EXODUS 15:2

"No other joy would last as long…"

As You deliver my children through the
"Red Seas" of this life, may they abide forever in
the joy of knowing that it is You alone, Oh! God,
who can save. And may You take joy in
the fact that they willingly received the strength
that Your mighty hand supplies.

"Thou wilt make known to me the path of life;
In Thy presence is fullness of joy;
In Thy right hand there are pleasures forever."

Psalm 16:11

"Father, calm their fear."

Oh! Lord God, when my children's hands shake
in fear, when their frightened hearts race out
of control, and when the cold sweat of
an anxious moment pours down their temples,
may You
settle their very spirits with the assurance that
You are close to them. And may that deep calm
be a sign of defeat to the enemy of their souls.

"The Lord is my light and my salvation,
Whom shall I fear?
The Lord is the defense of my life; Whom
shall I dread?"

PSALM 27:1

"Guide their feet, Lord, light their path..."

In their walk through time, may they realize
that You alone can see clearly what lies ahead.
Help me to show them that Your light is a
lamp only to their feet and beyond that,
they must trust You with the journey.
And may their feet be careful where they go!

"Thy word is a lamp to my feet,
and a light to my path."
PSALM 119:105

"May their eyes on You be cast..."

Oh! God, please help my children fix
their gaze upon You.
Give them the courage to look past the
temporal pleasures of this world and see
the immeasurable riches of Your
everlasting kingdom. And when they come
to a crossroads in their lives,
may they see only the Cross of Christ,
Your beloved Son. And may it remind
them to look only to You for their strength.

"My eyes are continually toward the Lord,
for He will pluck my feet out of the net."
PSALM 25:15

"Give their hands a kingdom task..."

Whatever their hands are called to do
within these walls of time, may it be
done to glorify Your holy cause.
Oh! God, deliver them from evil works
that would leave the stain of innocent blood
on their hands. Instead, help them to desire to
reach out to others with a heart of compassion.
And my their hands be raised often to You in
worship.

"Whatever your hand finds to do, verily, do it
with all your might..."

"I glorified Thee on the earth, having
accomplished the work which
Thou hast given me to do."
ECCLESIASTES 9:10 & JOHN 17:4

"A purpose for their years."

As long as they shall live, Oh! Lord,
grace my children's years with an awareness of
the heavenly purpose for their earthly existence.
May their lives not be wasted on the world.

"And we know that God causes all things to
work together for good to those who
love God, to those who are called
according to His purpose.
ROMANS 8:28

"And as my flesh cries out for bread..."

On this day, Oh! Lord, I come to your throne
bearing the offering of fleshly hunger.
In no way is this small sacrifice
comparable to what You gave to us in
Your Holy Son, Christ Jesus.
Still, I come with a hopeful heart that You
will see this hunger as a cry for Your
attentive ear.
Hear me, Oh! Lord.

"...Is not life more than food...?"
MATTHEW 6:25

"May I hunger, Lord, instead..."

Each time this fleshly hunger rises up
in me today and gnaws at my mind, crying
to be satisfied, I will refuse it and
be grateful for this momentary, bearable
pain. It will be the pin prick in my
soul that reminds me of the eternal
purpose for which I pray,
Oh! God, have mercy on my children!

"Blessed are those who hunger
and thirst for righteousness,
for they shall be satisfied."
MATTHEW 5:6

"That my children would be fed..."

Create, Oh! God, in my children's hearts,
a deep hunger to know You. Replace their
appetite for the temporal with a desire for the
things that will not pass away. May they come
to the table You have prepared for them, and
be grateful receivers of Your mercy and grace.

"Thou dost prepare a table before me
in the presence of my enemies..."
PSALM 23:5

"On Your words of life."

Your words, Oh! Lord, are flavored
with the sweetness of truth and life. Let my
children daily be sustained by Your food.
May the revelations of Your undeniable and
absolute truths serve to nourish both their
body and spirit until You come.
May Your presence in their lives
make their bones strong
so that they will walk with You
all the days of their lives.

"How sweet are Thy words to my taste!
Yes, sweeter than honey to my mouth!"
PSALM 119:103

"So...Father God, to You I come
In the name of Your Son
I bring my children to Your throne
Father, hear my cry."

Room To Write

The open pages that follow are for your use in organizing your prayer schedule as well as the petitions you will offer on behalf of your children. Please write legibly, keeping in mind that this will possibly become a written legacy of your love and prayers for your children.

Children's names

_____

_____

_____

Day chosen to concentrate prayers and fasting

_____

The two (or three) greatest desires I have for my children are:

1. _____

2. _____

3. _____

Room To Write
SPECIAL REQUESTS AND SPECIFIC NEEDS

Room To Write
SPECIAL REQUESTS AND SPECIFIC NEEDS

_____

_____

_____

_____

_____

_____

_____

_____

_____

_____

_____

_____

_____

_____

_____

_____

_____

_____

Room To Write

PRAYERS AND ANSWERS

_____

_____

_____

_____

_____

_____

_____

_____

_____

_____

_____

_____

_____

_____

_____

_____

_____

Room To Write
Scriptures that Encourage

_____

_____

_____

_____

_____

_____

_____

_____

_____

_____

_____

_____

_____

_____

_____

_____

Room To Write
NOTES TO MY CHILDREN

_____

_____

_____

_____

_____

_____

_____

_____

_____

_____

_____

_____

_____

_____

_____

_____

_____

Room To Write
Notes to My Children

_____

_____

_____

_____

_____

_____

_____

_____

_____

_____

_____

_____

_____

_____

_____

_____

_____

A Word From Annie

Though the emphasis of this book is the importance of the father's commitment to pray for his children, let me assure you that the mother's responsibility is by no means diminished. Instead, she must join with him in prayer. In cases where there is not a father who is actively involved in the children's lives, it is the mother who must step in and do a job that is really designed for two people. Caring for kids is a high calling for the woman. And included in the long list of things she must do for a child's welfare is spending time before the Lord on their behalf.

If the father of your children is responding to the "urgency" of prayer that Steve wrote about, he will need your support and encouragement. Your contribution is paramount. Keep in mind that the fervent prayers of a mother for her children are usually the subject of memorable quotes and acclaim. For example, Abraham Lincoln spoke affectionately of his mother's influence and publicly credited her with the accomplishments he had made in his life. When Apostle Paul wrote to Timothy (1 Timothy 1:5) he commended the young man for his sincere faith, which was the result of the spiritual influence of his mother, Eunice, and his grand-mother, Lois, on his life. And, of course, our Lord and Savior Jesus Christ was influenced by His mother, Mary, who had found great favor with God. And may I add that I will be forever grateful to Lillian Chapman, my mother-in-law, for her earnest investment of prayer into Steve's life. I am the benefactor of the devotion of a great woman. Without a doubt, there is no denying the incredible importance of a mother co-laboring on her knees in prayer with her husband. We cannot refuse to share the burden he has for the kids.

It is a tremendous blessing for me to see Steve's dili-gent involvement with our children. He has earned their respect as well as their trust that he will be there for them either in the flesh or on his knees. Several years ago, when he began to devote Wednesdays to praying for Nathan and Heidi, I decided to look for ways that I could quietly facilitate his efforts. The following are a list of things I have done to be of assistance. As a mother and wife, you will likely develop your own list of helpful con-tributions to his time of prayer. May God bless you abundantly as you do.

1. In our home, Wednesdays has become a regular focal point in our week. It is a day that we have learned to treat a little differently than all the other days of the week. At the beginning of the day of fasting, if I sense that they have forgotten, I try to remind the children that Steve is not eating. It should not always fall on the shoul-

ders of the one "doing without" to make that announcement. When we are traveling and its time for lunch, if I see the children struggling with the knowledge that they are eating and their father is not, I assure them that they are free to partake and that their dad will not be offended.

2. I try to avoid accepting social activities through the day on Wednesdays until the fast has ended. Steve has been careful to maintain a predictable schedule, which is very helpful to me in regards to planning.

3. To accommodate Steve's day of fasting, I don't cook a wonderful breakfast for the rest of the family on Wednesday mornings. He doesn't require that of me, its my choice. I save the "big breakfast" for another day. Instead, I stay with simple foods such as cereal or bagels. (I cannot tell you how many times I have forgotten it was Wednesday and prepared a family favorite.)

4. When the evening comes on Wednesday, I try to prepare a nice meal. The entire family comes together for a special dinner and to celebrate the breaking of the fast.

5. Finally, as often as I can, I join Steve on Wednesdays in his quest for the children's spiritual welfare. It is true that there are times when a mother should not participate in a fast, such as during a pregnancy or while nursing a child. A physician should be consulted in these cases before going without food. If, for some reason, I am unable to take part in the fast, I don't eliminate praying because the children need to see a united force of prayer on their behalf.

The effects of this type of devotion to the spiritual needs of our children are sometimes subtle. Though you may not readily detect the changes in their lives, continue on your course and do not cease to encourage your husband in his dedication. "Stand and see" what God will do through the simplicity of devotion to Christ in your prayers and fasting.

Someday, the children will verbalize their gratitude for the attention they received before the throne of God. Nathan, for example, has remarked that he has been tempted to do things he knows is wrong. Yet, he has resisted because he remembers "Wednesdays" and the investment his father is making into his life. Knowing that his dad is praying and fasting for him has made it easier to refuse the wrong and choose the right. I remember one day he called home from college on Wednesday. He told me he was having a rough day and asked, "Is dad praying for me today?" My response was, "Its Wednesday isn't it?" Enough was said.

Both of our kids have come to count on their dad's prayers. The following letter from Heidi expresses some of her thoughts about Steve's sacrifice on her behalf. Perhaps her words will encourage you as you consider joining us on a day like Wednesday.

"I didn't know about my dad's 'Wednesday's Prayer' until a few years ago. I was always at school while he was fasting during the day, so I had no idea.

When I found out that he had been fasting every Wednesday for me, I felt so honored and loved to have a dad that would care for me enough to do that every week. I look at Wednesdays in a whole different light. Before, I didn't really think about that day as anything other than just another 24 hours. But now, a Wednesday doesn't go by without me thinking about how much my daddy loves me! It makes me think of the blessing God has given me: faithful, God-fearing parents.

There's a comforting blanket that falls on my shoulders every Wednesday when I know that I'm being lifted up in prayer by one who truly loves me. I know that when I have children, I will be doing the same for them as my dad does for me. He has given me something to pass on-the power of prayer. I thank God for giving me the best parents in the world."

God bless you...and may God bless your children.

Annie

About The Author

Steve Chapman, along with his wife, Annie, have been singer/songwriters since the mid-1970's. Married in 1975 and based in the Nashville, Tennessee area, they have recorded over twenty albums and written eight books to date. With all they have accomplished in their years, each of them agree that their best work is Nathan and Heidi, their children.

Other books available from
Steve Chapman:

A Look At Life From A Deerstand
Harvest House Publishers

Full Draw
S & A Family, Inc.